How to Make Your Family Strong

God's purposes for parents and children in the Bible

by Mike Jelliffe
Illustrations by Bob Browne

How to Make Your Family Strong
by Mike Jelliffe

All rights reserved.
Copyright © 2025 Michael A Jelliffe

In accordance with copyright laws, this book or parts thereof may not be reproduced in any form, stored in an retrieval system, or transmitted in any form by any means - electronic, mechanical, photocopy, recording, or otherwise - without prior written permission of the publisher.

No AI Training: Without in any way limiting the author's exclusive rights under copyright, any use of this publication to "train" generative artificial intelligence (AI) technologies to generate text is expressly prohibited. The author reserves all rights to license uses of this work for generative AI training and development of machine learning language models.

Published by Nenge Books, Australia, 2024, June 2025
ABN 26809396184
nengebooks1@gmail.com
www.nengebooks.com
Illustrations © Bob Browne, Grass Roots Comic Co. Pty Ltd
Used by permission.

This retitled and updated edition was previously published in 1990 as "Strengthening the Christian Family", ISBN9980-61-142-1

ISBN 978-0-6484284-7-3

How to Make Your Family Strong

Contents

Page 3 - Introduction

Page 4 - God's Design in Marriage & Family

Page 9 - The Ideal of Marriage

Page 14 - Husband's and Wives

Page 21 - Children in the Family

Page 28 - Living as a Christian Family Today

Page 35 - Bibliography and further reading.

Page 36 - Discussion Questions

How to Make Your Family Strong

How to Make Your Family Strong

INTRODUCTION.

The aim of this course is to introduce you to aspects of being a Christian family that will strengthen you in your marriage and family life.

In Melanesia today there are lots of things which are trying to destroy Christian families, and we must recognise that Satan is throwing his arrows of destruction at the family, knowing that families are at the roots of community life. Destroy the family unit, and the community is destroyed. Yet God has created marriage and family life as His own unique way of blessing us in our earthly life, enabling us to draw closer to Him. Yet why do so many people find marriage and family life painful instead of pleasant, demanding instead of delightful, and a burden rather than a blessing?

We need to be reminded of all that God had in mind when He instituted marriage, and to understand afresh why marriage is so important in His sight. We need to be reminded that God is vitally interested in every aspect of our earthly welfare, and that includes family life (which takes a major portion of our time). We need to picture again the vision of an ideal marriage, and long for that just as we long for an ideal walk with our Lord. And lastly but not least, we must recognise the methods and tricks of Satan at work in our society today, display them for their true value, and learn to overcome them.

So in this book/course we will consider first of all God's Design in the Family - the reasons for family, and why families are so important in God's sight.

Secondly we will consider the Ideal of Marriage - what a marriage should be like.

Thirdly we will take a look at the roles and responsibilities of various family members - particularly husbands and wives.

The fourth chapter we will talk about children - their relationships with parents, discipline and discipling.

Then, lastly, we will consider the various forces and attitudes which are at work today in PNG trying to destroy our Christian values in the family.

At the back of the book you will find questions for discussion. Use them for discussion and learning if you are studying this book in a group, chapter by chapter, for example.

How to Make Your Family Strong

GOD'S DESIGN IN MARRIAGE AND FAMILY.

1. The Creation of the sexes - man and woman.

Bible ref: Genesis 1:26-31, 2:7-25.

The Bible has much to say about marriage and family life, but if we are to discover the true meaning of marriage, we must turn back to the book of Genesis. The first two chapters of Genesis give us the story of the creation of the world and everything in it.

On the sixth day God created a man (Adam) and a woman (Eve) as the pinnacle of His creation. Unfortunately, when Satan tempted Eve and Adam, and sin came into the world when the disobeyed God, the scene changed. However, there are four things we can note from this story:

(1) When God had created man and woman He was VERY pleased with His work, and delighted in them. Gen 1:21, at the completion of the creation of everything else on the earth, "God saw that it was good". But in 1:31, His reaction to His creation with the addition of Adam and Eve was "it was **very** good".

(2) Man and woman were created different to all the other elements or beings of creation because they were uniquely created in the image of God. Genesis 1:26 "then God said ' Let us make man in Our image, according to our likeness...'". Man is not the same as the animals. He has capacities of heart, soul, spirit, and creativity which are uniquely his because he is made in the image of God.

How to Make Your Family Strong

(3) God created man first, and then the woman (Genesis 2:7-25). God saw that Adam needed a helpmate, a companion, someone to share this beautiful creation with, so He created the woman 'out of the man'. Adam's delight is expressed in Genesis 2:23 - "Wow! Here is someone just like me, bone of my bone, flesh of my flesh".

(4) In the story of Adam and Eve we see God's true perspective on marriage - one man and one woman in complete union. Genesis 2:24- "For this reason a man shall LEAVE his father and mother, and shall CLEAVE to his wife; and they shall become ONE FLESH." This verse indicates a threefold process in marriage.

(a) Leaving parents.

In marriage a couple begin their own family unit, and separate from their parents.

(b) Cleaving to partner.

To cleave means to stick together faithfully, as if glued together - the husband's interests become the wife's, the wife's interests become the husband's; they share their lives together.

(c) Complete Union - one flesh.

This is more than just sexual union, but that is included. The sexual union makes them to be one body, but 'one flesh' indicates a union in all aspects of life in the physical realm.

The church in Liberia gives to newly marrieds a wooden carved chain, with carved figureheads of a man and a woman at each end to remind them of this. Though each is a separate carving, each is carved from the same block of wood, and remains attached to the other. The chain has no links because it is carved as a chain, similar to the three-legged tables carved from one block of wood that we see sometimes here in PNG.

Author Walter Trobisch, in his excellent book *'I Married You'* (which I would recommend you read) uses the picture of a triangle to illustrate this - three points marked 'leaving', 'cleaving' and 'one flesh'. I will mention this only briefly here, but we will come back to consider build on this later on. See the diagram on page 8.

In summary then we could say that mankind was created to occupy a special place in the heart of God, for he was created in the likeness and image of God. Woman was created from man for the specific purpose

How to Make Your Family Strong

of intimate companionship and love, and God's stated intent is that a **monogamous, heterosexual** family unit is His design. Jesus also mentioned this verse (Mark 10:9), adding that this union is sanctioned by God **for life**.

2. God's Purposes in the family.

(1) I believe that God has placed marriage as the highest example of human relationship that we can experience, and that through a successful, happy marriage we can learn more about Him in a real life setting than is possible anywhere else. Within a marriage, each partner has the potential to develop a relationship which is deeper than any other, except perhaps his or her relationship with God Himself. Within a marriage, and only within true marriage, each person has the capability to minister to his or her partner in a way which is nothing short of an expression of God's own ministry - in other words, each partner has within marriage the potential to be Christ to his or her partner in a way that is not possible with any other person

(2) Marriage provides fulfillment in life for each partner as he or she develops in union with their spouse, offering the love and companionship that each person needs.

(3) Procreation - marriage is the institution which God designed for FULFILLED sexual union, so that children would be born and the human race multiplied. (Genesis 1:28).

(4) Families provide the framework for children to be raised in love and discipline, the ideal place for them to be educated and equipped for all aspects of their future adult life - physical, social, moral and spiritual.

(5) God has instituted marriage to illustrate many key truths that He wishes us to learn. Here are several:

☐ The unity of the Godhead - the fact of the Trinity is plainly stated in the Bible, even in Genesis 1:26, where God said "Let US make man in OUR image..." We do not understand how the three Persons of God can live in total unity and harmony. If God had made us as all men, we would never be able to know. But through the marriage relationship we can draw closer to one other person in a relationship which should be closer to a united, harmonious relationship than any other we could experience. In this sense, marriage can provide the closest illustration on earth to the true unity that exists between the Father, Son and Holy Spirit. This is a true love relationship.

☐ Jesus instructed us to pray to *"Our Father in heaven."* (Matthew 6:9). In other places too the Bible speaks of God as our heavenly Father.

How to Make Your Family Strong

Within the family, the father is a continual reminder to us of God the Father. Within a family as well, children can learn more about God through their relationship with their father than any other single factor.

- [ ] In the New Testament (eg.Ephesians 5:22-32) the marriage illustration is used, and Jesus is the Groom, the church His Bride. We are not to look at marriage here on earth and liken the Great Marriage to that, but to use the marriage of Jesus and His Church as our model or example. Our marriages will only ever be a shadow or forerunner of the greatest marriage that will ever be. Not only that, but we can learn from the Groom and Bride how to behave in our own marriages.

- [ ] Eve was created to be a helper and companion for Adam. Likewise Jesus promised in John 14 to send the Holy Spirit, the Helper or Counsellor - in the Greek the 'parakletos', literally the one who is called alongside to strengthen and help (from Greek *para-kaleo*). I believe that within marriage, the role of the woman in support of her husband can help us understand better the ministry of the Holy Spirit, and perhaps is even a human illustration of the spiritual ministry of the Holy Spirit.

- [ ] God is creative. He alone has the power to create something from nothing. Part of His image that we have been given is the ability to be creative, though we can only express this within the created world. The closest we can come to true creativity is expressed in marriage in the desire of a couple to have children. In animals it is the result of natural urges and behaviour. In people it is ultimately the expression of God's creativity within us, which finds fullfilment within marriage. The joy that a man and his wife discover in childbirth is a picture to us of the delight God has in us, His children.

There are no doubt other truths that we can find in Scripture about the model of marriage, but these points will be enough to focus our attention on the fact that God has ordained marriage, and has wonderfully blessed us in many ways by doing so. In the modern world, where marriage is treated so lightly, it does us well to realize again that God is at the heart of marriage and family life. To many of you, many of the points I have mentioned will be new thoughts for you.

Satan is determined to draw us away from God's ideal of marriage, and has very successfully managed to corrupt and destroy much that society and the church has held as sacred in marriage. <u>Love</u>, true love as demonstrated by Christ, has been distorted to mean sex. The idea of a <u>wedding</u> (whether traditional or western) recognised by the family, the community and God has given way to an 'all priviledges but no

How to Make Your Family Strong

responsibility' approach to just living together. The true value in sex as an expression of love, commitment and faithfulness to one partner, has become just a selfish meeting of one's own animal desires. Thus the three corners of the triangle have been broken, and nothing remains but broken people, searching for meaning in relationship, but unable to find it in what they know should be the best of relationships, but is not.

We as Christians must hold tightly to all that God has given us in marriage. It is our showpeice to the world - for a good marriage is a bold testimony to all that God desires for all men and women, a demonstration that two people can walk together in harmony and in love, that lifelong commitment to faithfulness to another person is possible, and that the blessings and benefits of such a relationship will not be given up for something else. And if all this is possible with another person, how much more with God.

The Marriage Triangle Diagram:

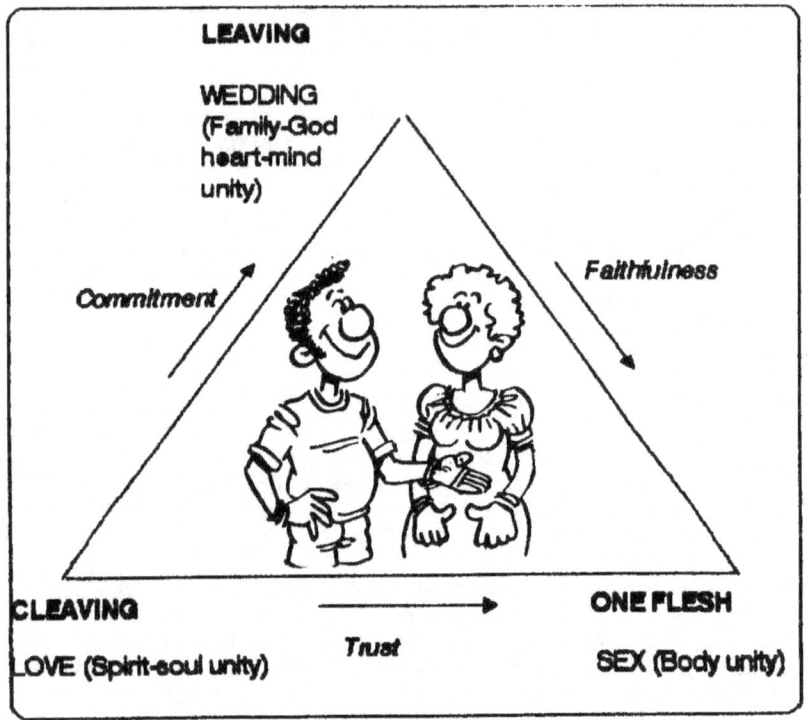

How to **Make Your Family Strong**

THE IDEAL OF MARRIAGE.

1. Christ and the Church.

Bible ref: Ephesians 5:21-33, Revelation 19:1-9.

In everything in life we learn so much better when we can follow someone elses example. This is especially true for the Christian, and our example is Christ Himself, who Peter says,"left an example for you to follow in His steps." (1 Peter 2:21). Though Peter was specifically referring to Christ's suffering, the Bible also tells us that Jesus has left us an example to follow in marriage too. Jesus is pictured as the Bridegroom, the Church as His Bride, and their wedding is to be the greatest event in the history of the universe - when Jesus returns to earth and takes to Himself for eternity those who have been faithfully preparing themselves for Him.

The relationship between Jesus and the Church then is the ideal from which we view our own marriages. We look first to Christ, then to our own situation, and not the other way round. Our own marriages are weak and in danger of failing, but His marriage is strong and secure. It is not even that His is an example of the best marriage - His IS the perfect marriage, and ours can only ever be in the shadow of that perfection. When we read of Christ's behaviour to the Church we are not just reading of one way that a husband can behave to his wife, we are reading of the ONLY way. When we read of the Churches attitude to Christ, we are not reading of one way a wife should act, we are reading of the ONLY way - if you want your marriage to be a success.

In the next chapter, roles & responsibilities of HUSBANDS AND WIVES, we will look specifically at the model of Christ and the Church and see specifically the behaviour modelled by Jesus and His Bride. However there are several key points which we need to establish firmly in our minds first about God's ideal of marriage.

(a) Faithfulness

We might ask the question, 'How many brides does Jesus have?' At once we realize that it is a stupid question, for there is only one answer - one. The Church worldwide is the Bride of Christ.

Faithfulness is one of the foundations upon which God has built His Covenant relationship with man. It is a basic characteristic of God's nature that He is faithful - He will perform the task or keep the promise He has indicated. It is also one of the foundations of covenant in marriage.

How to Make Your Family Strong

Nowhere else do we see this illustrated as vividly as in the Book of Hosea, in the OT. God called the prophet Hosea to marry Gomer, who turned out to be a harlot, and unfaithful to her husband. The picture of Hosea's love for Gomer, and his faithfulness to her, is in stark contrast to her unfaithfulness in marriage. It is no accident that God called Hosea to demonstrate true faithfulness in the context of marriage, for relationship in marriage is a mirror of relationship with God. *Gomer is a picture of the Israelite people who were following pagan gods and not the Lord. Hosea is a picture of God faithfully seeking to restore their relationship.*

(b) Life Commitment.

Covenant faithfulness is a contract between two people to join only to the other person in the context of their relationship. In marriage that means a commitment to seek the best for the other person, to love and support them, until death cancels the contract. Jesus reiterated this clearly in Mark 10:9-12, *"What God has joined together, let no man separate,"* followed by His statement that anyone divorcing and remarrying commits adultery. Paul followed up in Romans 7:1-3.

(c) Monogamy

Perhaps we could ask another question, "How many wives did God give Adam?" Again the answer is one. Eve was created as the perfect wife for Adam. God set the pattern of monogamy (one wife, one husband) with Adam and Eve. Only within the context of a monogamous marriage can true faithfulness exist. Jesus stated plainly that *"the TWO shall become ONE"* (Mtt.19), and Paul taught that *"every man should have his own wife, and every wife her own husband"*. (1 Cor. 7:2). Paul also said that church leaders should have only one wife.

How to Make Your Family Strong

Certainly many of the OT men had several wives, but we must see this in the light of man's sinful nature causing him to turn aside from God's plan. It also caused them many heartaches and problems. On one hand we may say they have set us an example. However, it is probably better for us to consider their examples as warnings to us.

In PNG today polygamy is still practiced. However, it seems to be predominantly associated with a desire for increased status and power within the community. Unfortunately a new type of polygamy, popular in the western world, is also becoming popular. This is sometimes called *successive* polygamy, where a man or a woman may have a series of wives or husbands, though there is a marriage and subsequent divorce each time. Again, this is contrary to the whole purpose of God, and renders the concept of covenant faithfulness as meaningless.

2. Divorce and re-marriage.

When we consider the idea of faithfulness in a life long commitment that we have talked about already, we can appreciate that divorce is against God's plan - as Jesus said, *"man cannot separate what God has joined"* (Matt 19:6). He then went on specifically to say ,*"whoever divorces his wife, ... and marries another, commits adultery".*

In Malachi 2:13-16 God speaks out very clearly about His feelings about divorce. *"I hate divorce,"* He says, saying that He has been *"a witness between you and the wife of your youth, against whom you have dealt treacherously, though she is your companion and your wife by covenant".* Again God reminds us that marriage is a covenant relationship - it is not designed to be broken.

Paul spells this out even more clearly in Romans 7:1-3 and 1 Cor.7:39 - to marry someone else while your first partner is alive is adultery. The problem today is that divorce has become so common that we have forgotten that it is not God's plan. Just as a dripping tap wears away the cement underneath it, so constant exposure to sin in marriage has caused us to forget God's way.

Even amongst Christians in the western world divorce has become acceptable. But it is not acceptable to God. Why? Because in divorce we are saying that the problems we encountered in our marriage were too great, and as Christians we are saying in effect that God is not big enough to handle our marriage problems, or solve them. Divorce amongst Christians is really just a testimony to the world that God is NOT able to help you to live how He wants.

How to Make Your Family Strong

3. Failure and Forgiveness.

Of course, it is easy to condemn divorce if you have not lived through it, and many people around the world today, including PNG, bear the scars of divorce. The wounds may heal, but the scars still remain. So we need to be reminded that adultery and fornication and divorce are not unforgiveable sins. The unforgiveable sin is to reject and so grieve the Holy Spirit - to refuse to submit yourself to Him and allow Him to minister to you. We are all sinners, and sin is sin, whether it is adultery of the heart or adultery in the body, or whether it is adultery in our relationship with God - turning aside to follow idols. God forgives, and it is in these areas of life where we can really be hurting that God wants to reveal His love and forgiveness to us in a new way. He also wants this **love and forgiveness that He shows us to be the basis for our relationship to our marriage partner.**

God is also a God of new beginnings, and in terms of marriage, when we are prepared to lay our past sins at the foot of the Cross, acknowledging our failure, He is able to restore to us "the years the locusts have destroyed". I have seen couples who were divorced as non-christians, but who after coming to know Christ became reunited in marriage again. I also know folk whose marriages broke up when they were non-christians, and since becoming Christians they have remarried Christian partners.

Jesus said to the woman caught in adultery (John 8:11) *"Neither do I condemn you, go and sin no more"*. When we feel guilty about sins in this area of our life, we are the ones who condemn ourselves, not God. **Jesus' forgiveness is complete, just as His death on the Cross was complete.** Of course Satan loves to tell us we are sinners, but God's forgiveness is greater than Satan's lies.

Walter Trobisch, in the book 'I Married You', has a beautiful story of a girl called Fatma. She was an African girl in Africa living with an expatriate who would not marry her. She came to a cricis point in her life and is ready to commit suicide by jumping off a bridge. Trobisch finds her at 3 am, and talks with her about Christ and forgiveness. She confesses to having at least 6 men, and abortions. At the same time a man called Maurice is desperately looking for a wife. Yet he is not wanting an older woman because he wants a virgin. So as a 33 yr.old he is looking for a schoolgirl as a wife. During the true story, the Lord tells Maurice that Fatma is to be his wife. At that stage he had never seen her before, and knew none of her background.

As Trobisch and his wife leave the city by plane after lecturing there, he comments to his wife, "Poor Maurice, he so much wanted to marry a virgin. And he ends up with Fatma".

How to Make Your Family Strong

His wife contradicts him. "But she is a virgin. She has been cleansed - as the Bride of Christ, as the Bible says, without spot, without blemish, without wrinkle".

Indeed, says Trobisch, his wife was right.

If Jesus Christ forgives you, He takes away the guilt and shame of past experiences, even if He cannot make your body new again. You cannot undo the past, but you can live the future free from guilt and shame.

4. The Marriage Triangle (diagram page 8)

One way of looking at marriage is the triangle concept, made popular by Walter Trobisch. When we look at the triangle concept of marriage, we see God's plan of progression in marriage. When the three corners are balanced, a marriage is happy.

The way to enter marriage is not through the SEX corner. Many who have rushed into sex before marriage have found it does not work. Sex is more than just a bodily function - it is bound up in emotion and faith commitment to the other person. The result is guilt, shame, disappointment, and even hatred on the inside, and perhaps venereal disease or AIDS. Sex is more than just the touching of two bodies. It is the touching of the two spirits as well, and so it cannot be fulfilling and satisfying unless there is a unity in spirit.

Similarly, those who will not enter properly through the WEDDING corner, but marry against family and community approval, and God's approval, and enter into a relationship of 'de-facto' marriage, or convenience marriage, suffer because there is no covenant commitment, and so no trust.

The ideal is to enter through the corner of LOVE, developing a relationship of commitment to eachother, which is then expressed in a wedding. When sexual fulfillment follows on from these first two, then the triangle is complete. Unity of spirit, soul, heart and mind, and body, results - the three-cornered tent is a perfect shelter (see diagram on page 8).

How to **Make Your Family Strong**

HUSBANDS & WIVES

1. The Goal of Oneness.

In marriage we seek after a deep experience of personal intimacy through a relationship with a person of the opposite sex. The goal of marriage is really nothing less than complete oneness, or unity, in spirit, soul and body, and we see this clearly as God's stated intent in Genesis 2.

Adam and Eve enjoyed a oneness in the Garden of Eden (they were naked and not ashamed) which they lost when they sinned. Unfortunately, the results of sin have spoilt the marriage relationship ever since. Adam and Eve enjoyed not only a unity in their own relationship, but a closeness with God which they (and all mankind) lost when the sinned. In the Garden, all their needs were met - life was totally fulfilled in God's presence. Out of the Garden, their needs were not met. It was hard work to provide food, toiling in the ground, and it would be hard work to live up to all that God desired in other areas of life.

2. Our needs for Security and Significance.

Each of us has needs. Clothing, shelter and food are basic human needs, which we could call physical needs. We also have basic personal needs, and these can be summarized as security and significance, or love and acceptance by other people.

(a) Security.

No one is an island, alone in the world and isolated from everyone else. One of our basic needs is to feel that we are loved and accepted. Crabb defines it as "a convinced awareness of being unconditionally and totally loved without needing to change on order to win love, loved by a love that is freely given, that cannot be earned and therefore cannot be lost". (p.29) In the Garden this need was totally met by God Himself, but out of the Garden, one of the results of sin and the cutting off of man's relationship with God has been man's need to rediscover love and hence, security.

(b) Significance.

Each of us also has a need to know that we are making an impact on someone elses life, that we are in fact useful to someone else. Crabb defines it as "a realisation that I am engaged in a responsibility or job that is truly important, whose results will not evaporate with time but will

How to Make Your Family Strong

last through eternity, that fundamentally involves having a meaningful impact on another person, a job for which I am completely adequate".(p.29) This means finding one's identity in relation to others, until which we do not feel we are a worthwhile person.

3. Fulfillment in marriage - just a dream ?

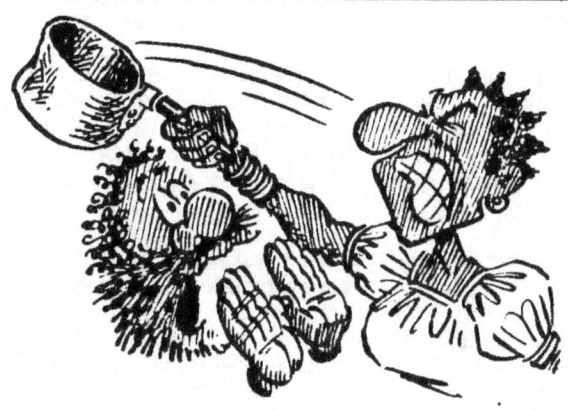

If God has designed marriage with love and companionship primarily in mind, then we should be able to find fulfillment of these personal needs within marriage. Typically in marriage though, we see the effects of sin holding us back from really discovering these needs being met, and the result is frustration and disappointment. A husband will wait until he feels his wife has met his needs for security and significance before he feels able to open himself to her, and the wife will do the same. We realize that each partner has what is needed to meet the other person's needs, but we hang back waiting for the other person to respond to us first. *The result is that we actually withhold from our partner the very love and support they need, and actively destroy the relationship.*

We have discovered in the process that marriage, the very thing we thought would meet our deepest needs, is keeping us from really having those needs met. That is the root cause of much frustration in marriage, and many separations and divorces. The person we married who we expected would meet our deepest needs is not able to do so, and we are unfulfilled.

How to Make Your Family Strong

4. How can our needs be met ?

There are 4 ways we can look at:

(a) <u>Ignore them</u> - If you don't eat food, you die physically. If your personal needs for acceptance and love are not being met, you die as a person. Many people are dying from boredom and emptiness feelings, and have turned to drugs or alcohol as a result of feeling worthless as a person.

(b) <u>Achievement in work</u> - many look to their work or other interests to satisfy their deepest personal needs - sport, work, politics, even church, can provide avenues for people to try to discover love and acceptance. But these needs have been implanted by God and can never be fulfilled by activity, no matter how good it may be. Only satisfying relationships will meet these needs.

(c) <u>Through marriage</u> - This looks good in theory. Each person clinging to the other to find their personal needs met perfectly. However, in practice, in marriage we only find that we closer we come to our partner, the more we discover they cannot meet our deepest needs. Herein lies the basic problem to our approach to marriage - *we are approaching it from a standpoint of selfishness, seeking for someone who can meet our needs*. We become like leeches on eachother, trying to have our own needs met like drawing blood from the other person. We feel great disappointment when our partner lets us down.

Yet it is possible to have our needs for personal worth met fully, and marriage if it does nothing else should drive us to discover where we can find fulfillment, having shown us that it is *not* to be found within marriage.

(d) <u>Depend on the Lord</u> - God has provided in Christ for us everything we need, and it is in Christ and only in Christ that we will find true love and true worth. God's acceptance of us is complete (Romans 5:8; 15:7; 8:1). His love is freely given to us, and in His love alone will we find true security.

He has given each one of us a task in His body (Eph.2:10), and we will find no greater expression of being worthwhile than in ministering to others according to God's plan. We find all our needs for significance met totally in God.

How to Make Your Family Strong

5. Spirit Oneness.

Once we realize that in Christ all our personal needs are met, it not only encourages us to seek to know Christ better, that we might work out our experience in a deeper relationship with Christ, but it frees us to see marriage in it's proper context - that of ministry. Whereas our earlier goal was to manipulate (or use to our advantage) our partner so that he or she would meet our needs, now that we understand those personal needs are all met in Christ, we are free to concentrate on meeting our partners needs.

Whereas our eternal worth is in Christ, it is true that God uses marriage now to develop in each of us a conscious awareness of our personal worth. Christ grants us our security and worth, but it is through our husband or wife that we feel it, as we minister love and acceptance from a position of security in Christ.

Security and significance come from God, but are felt through our marriage partner.

Herein lies the wonderful ministry potential that we can have to our in our marriages. We turn to the Lord for satisfaction of deepfelt personal needs for security and satisfaction, but we turn to each other for ministry, to feel security and significance. *We are accepted and loved by Christ, that is the fact, but the expression of that, the feeling, comes through our marriage partner. This* is Spirit Oneness - two people seeking God together.

6. Soul Oneness.

If our deepest needs are met in Christ, then we are free to turn our attention unselfishly to our spouse. This is the basis of true love, which is essentially a preoccupation with the others needs. This is the model that Jesus set - *"greater love has no man than this, that he lay down his life for his friends"* - is the basis for all submission (Ephesians 5:21), *thinking of the other person first.* Crabb says,"Husbands and wives are to regard marriage as an opportunity to minister in a unique and special way to another human being, to be used of God to bring their spouses into a more satisfying appreciation of their worth as persons who are secure and significant in Christ." (p.52).

There are three things one must do to move from the worldly standard of manipulation (getting) to ministry (giving) in marriage:

(a) Decide to minister to, not manipulate, your partner;

(b) Be aware of your partner's needs,

How to **Make Your Family Strong**

(c) Realize you are God's chosen person to meet those needs.

None of this is possible without *communication*. When two people are

not getting on well, the thing that suffers first is communication. A wife gets upset, so she refuses to talk to her husband. Or a wife expresses disapproval of her husband's activities, so he refuses to tell her any more about them. So barriers are created. It is impossible to know your partner's needs unless you have some communication, and the better the communication, the better the understanding and so ministry possible.

Communication is both talking and listening. (The book *Christian Marriage and Family Life*, by Ian Malins, CBM, has two excellent studies on this, studies 13 & 14).

7. Body Oneness.

God created sex, and it is part of His plan for you and I to find fulfillment in life by enjoying sex. However, Satan has perverted sex to the extent that many people do not even know how it should be used properly. Fun sex, as offered by Satan, may give a momentary pleasure, but soon after brings pain and guilt and shame. God's intention
was that sex be part of marriage, and only within marriage will we find fulfillment in it.
If we isolate sex from spirit and soul oneness, then it becomes empty actions, feels good to the body (for a short while), but has no meaning for the person.

How to Make Your Family Strong

If we consider the triangle concept, (see diagram page 8) sex in isolation from the other two corners of leaving and uniting is similarly meaningless - one corner cannot stand on it's own. However, within marriage and the context of spirit and soul oneness that already exist, when two odies housing two persons who are already one come together physically, there is total fulfillment and happiness.

8. How can we Minister then ?

If we look at the diagram of the relationship between Christ and the Church (next page) we can see various roles and responsibilities highlighted.
By doing these things we will actually be ministering to our partners, making them feel more secure and significant.

The theory of this may sound good, but we need to actively be looking

at ways of putting it into action. This is the hard part! For example, whenever a situation of conflict comes up between a couple, they may

well find a solution is nearby if they are prepared to seriously ask themselves, "Am I manipulating my husband or wife, or ministering to him or her?" To then change their behaviour to ministry will solve the problem. When we consider such aggressive or violent behaviour as wife-beating which is common in PNG, we begin to realise that we have gone a long way from God's ideal of *ministy* within marriage.

How to Make Your Family Strong

Key Scriptures: Ephesians 5, Colossians 3.

Male picture

JESUS

Head & Saviour   Groom & Husband

Prepared in sacrificial LOVE (Eph 5:25)

Lead (Eph 5:23)   Nourish, feed and care (Eph 5:29)
Serve (Eph 5:23)   Cherish, nurture in the Lord (Eph 5:26-27)
Purify (Titus 2:14)   Love as own body, give up self (Eph 5:25,33)
                        Love, not harsh (Col 3:19)

A covenant commitment with God (Mark 14:24-25; Malachi 2:14-15; Eph 5:31-32)
Faithfulness until death (Romans 7:1-3; Matthew 19:3-9)
Forgiveness (Ephesians 4:32) & Trust (John 14:1)

Conjugal rights* (1Cor 7:3-5)

Respect (Eph 5:33)
Accept authority** (Eph 5:23; Titus 2:15)
Submit *(put the other's needs first)* (Eph 5:24)
Follow.

Prepared in purity & holiness (Eph 5:27; Rev 19:7-8)

Body   Bride & Wife

CHURCH

Female picture

*Conjugal rights are the rights to intimacy within marriage, rights not offered outside of marriage.
**'Obey' as a command is never used in the Bible of the relationship of wife to husband. Submission to another person's authority is not so they can selfishly "lord it over" the person (Matthew 20:25), it is so that the person can receive the goodness and blessing of the person in authority as they come under that person's welfare. Submission is willingly recognising the person in authority's mandate to serve.

How to Make Your Family Strong

CHILDREN IN THE FAMILY

1. When there are no children.

(a) God's plan.

Before we look at the roles and responsibilities of children and parents within a family, we must pause to consider couples who have no children. Many couples find that after a period of time they have been unable to have children. Does this mean their marriage is not complete, or they should now separate?

When we consider the key passage of Genesis 2:24 again, we discover that children are not mentioned. God's primary purpose in marriage is for fulfillment in union for two people, that in discovering a joy in partnership together they might learn to appreciate the partnership that God seeks to establish with them. It is not primarily to have children. At the same time, God's command was to multiply and populate the earth, so raising children is part of God's plan for couples.

In some parts of PNG, it is the custom for a couple to try to have a child before they marry. If a child is born, then they marry officially, if not, it is felt the wife is not a good wife, and they separate. What they have done in fact is enter marriage triangle through the sex corner, with commitment becoming dependent on children. In some places if the wife does not have children, then it is a reason for the husband to divorce the wife.

(b) Reasons for barrenness.

There are many reasons for a wife not being able to conceive. Sometimes sickness or disease (Sexually Transmitted Diseases) can damage the vital organs of the man or the woman so that they become sterile, and unable to produce children. Sometimes the man or the woman may have deformities in their bodies and internal tubes which prevent pregnancy. Other times it may be that they just need to understand better how their bodies function. For example, there are only certain times each month when the woman's body is able to conceive. If a man and wife do not have relations during this time, she will not become pregnant. It is easy to obtain books or advise on these matters from a Health clinic or Family Planning Centre.

Many couples who have not been able to have children have, after visiting a doctor or counsellor, found that, after a small operation or a better understanding of how their bodies function, they have been able to have children. Some though will never be able to have children. This

How to Make Your Family Strong

may be because the man or the woman cannot, and we must be careful not to blame the woman all the time. We must also realize that to have sexual relations outside marriage with other partners may expose us to STD which may mean we cannot have children later on - a big price to pay for a 5 minute experience!

In one part of New Ireland some years ago, the population was shown to be decreasing because so many women were becoming sterile after contracting gonorrhoea!!

So, although children are a part of God's plan for a couple in marriage, a marriage is still complete without children, and a couple can still find complete fulfillment in marriage without children. When we consider the marriage triangle again, we see the children as in the centre of the triangle - the fruit of a complete triangle.

2. The Purpose of Children.

(a) A Gift of God.

Psalm 127 makes it very clear that children are a gift from God, and that to be able to have children is to experience God's blessing. There are several cases in the OT when women who were unable to have children finally conceived through God's intervention (eg. Sarah and Hanah) and bore children. They had no doubt that these children were God's gifts! However, all who have children should see them as a cause for praise to God for His blessing in this way.

(b) An expression of creativity.

Children are an expression of the creativity that God has given us, the ability to create someone from "nothing", and so are the peak of achievement for a couple. In sexual union a couple can find fulfillment in expressing their love for eachother, and so when this expression bears the fruit of conception and childbirth, God's blessing is experienced. How this makes us realize the need for sexual union to be contained within the sphere of a love relationship in marriage.

(c) To continue the human race.

Children are God's way of ensuring the continuation of the human race - in fact, all of creation has been created on the basis of a male and female union to produce offspring. Only in people is this union not just a matter of instinctive behaviour, but an expression of love and commitment.

How to Make Your Family Strong

3. Raising Children

(a) Babies and young children.

Babies and young children are generally cared for most of the time by their mothers. Not only for their food and nourishment (breast milk), but God has given mothers a special bond with their babies. It is fostered by touch and feeling, and babies need to be held often to give them a sense of security and well-being.

In experiments with young monkeys, scientists have found that monkeys growing up with wire-frame substitutes for mothers (with a bottle) were unable to cope socially later in life compared to those growing up with the warmth and feel of their true mother.

I have been impressed with the way PNG men will often hold their little babies and young children too. It is something western men tend to feel ashamed to do. But a young child learns security from his father, and it is important that both a mother and father play a role in caring for their young children.

It is in the first five years of it's life that a child develops the patterns of behaviour and understanding of life and relationships that it will carry through the rest of it's life. If a child was not wanted, and the attitude of the parents when it was in conception and born was one of rejection, that child will grow up feeling constant rejection, and have problems as an adult, unless the Lord brings healing to that area.

It is no wonder then that children that are left to other people to care for, while they go to work, have problems later in life adjusting and fitting into society. It is not so bad here in PNG where relatives who live in the same house are available, but in western society, many children spend many hours a day in day care centres.

(b) School age children.

Whereas children learn most of the behaviour patterns and feelings in the first 5 years of life, school age years are a time for them to prove what they have learnt, and put it into practice. This time can be very frustrating for parents, and they can often feel like giving up! Certainly it causes many tensions and fights as children test their parents to see how far they can go to disobey them, and so on. They want to discover where the end of the leg rope is! My children, when told not to touch something, would extend one finger and place it about a mm from the object, and watch me. At times they would get too close and touch it, and then learn that disobience has a price to pay!

How to **Make Your Family Strong**

The thing that we as parents need to realize is that it is important for them to discover their boundaries. A child in a field will run straight to the boundary fence to see what's over it. They are learning what life is about, and where it's boundaries are. Then they have to learn to stick within those boundaries.

Why is this so important for Christians? Because if children grow up without realizing that in all of life there are boundaries, then they will stray across into Satan's area, and we will be powerless to stop them.

4. Discipline.

God has given us the responsibility of caring for our children, who we must remember are a gift from Him, so that we can teach them to find Him. The most important thing you can teach your child is to love God. Yes, it is important that I teach my child how to dress himself, how to brush his teeth, how to ride a bicycle, or make a fire, or build a canoe, or whatever, but if I, as a Christian parent, do not do all I can to teach my child to love God, then I have failed. That teaching does not come in speaking, but in demonstrating.

When I discipline my child and show him that we have rules and boundaries which cannot be broken or crossed without punishment, I am teaching him that God too has boundaries, that there is behaviour that is acceptable to Him and behaviour that is not, there is belief that God accepts, and there is belief and worship which He does not. I am in effect teaching my child in the context of home that there is a right and a wrong. Many children today are growing up with so little discipline that they do not know the difference between right and wrong. And when a person cannot tell when he is sinning, he feels that he has no need of a Saviour.

You see, many of the things we should be doing in our homes are really designed to help our children better relate to God when they grow up.

When a father will not take up his responsibility with his family, and will not relate to his children or discipline them, the child grows up without really understanding what the Bible means when it tells him God is his

How to Make Your Family Strong

Father. But when a father has spent time with his children and acted responsibly to them, disciplining them, giving them the security and love they need, then it is easy for those children to appreciate and respond to God when He says He is their Heavenly Father.

Many children in our towns and cities today are roaming around the streets while their fathers are out drinking and enjoying themselves. A father recently told me he could not bring himself to spank his child, but wondered why his two boys were disobedient. These boys had discovered their father was weak in this area, so they knew they could do whatever they wanted and he would not discipline them.

Unfortunately violence as discipline is common in PNG. We must consider the appropriateness of the discipline we use, but any form of violence towards another person is no longer acceptable in society or as a form of punishment.

We must remember that that discipline seeks *to bend the child's will without breaking their spirit* - not damaging them physically.

But as a child grows, others ways of discipline become necessary. It is not appropriate or proper for a father to smack a 16 yr. old daughter - though I know it happens! We find that for our older children, we can discipline them by withholding priveledges, and at the same time reward them for achievement if that is needed. We need to differentiate between deliberate disobedience, learning mistakes, and being aggravated purely because of inconvenience to ourselves. We need to give our children a climate where they need not be afraid of making mistakes in learning, yet in which they understand clearly the rules.

For example, when I was a teenager, my parents would let me go out at night with some friends to a party or something on the condition that I returned by 9pm. To have stayed out to 11pm deliberately would have meant next time I asked to go out, they said no. On the other hand, if I was back by 9 pm, next time they might say 9.30pm. I was too old for smacking, but still young enough to need guidance and discipline.

<u>Hebrews 12:3-11</u> - These verses give us some insight into the value of discipline.

Firstly, discipline should be administered in love. Too often we lash out at our kids and slap them for some action which angers us, and we feel we are disciplining them. But we are not. If you are angry, then it is best for you to cool down for a while first. Then take the child to a place where you are alone and let the child know what he has done wrong, and the

punishment being received. Don't let the child think you are angry at him - all he will learn is that Daddy blows his stack when I do something wrong. *Jeremiah 10:24*

God does not like some of the things we do, and they make him angry, but He loves us. His discipline is to teach us not to do those things, not because he hates us. In fact, it is because He loves us so much that He wants us to learn not to do those things! So too when we discipline our children, it should be in a spirit of love and not anger.

Secondly, the results of discipline are respect (that's what the father I talked about earlier wanted but didn't have) and the "peaceful fruit of righteousness" (knowing the right way to live) - and with God's discipline, holiness. Sure, it is painful for the child and the parents to discipline, but the fruits of it are worth it.

Proverbs has some good advise on discipline - read 13:1; 15:20; 23:13-14; 13:24 for example. The story of Samson is also a good example of the problems resulting from a lack of discipline (Judges 13-16).

How to Make Your Family Strong

5. Parent and Child responsibilities.

The Bible is quite clear with several statements about responsibilities in several areas, so we must consider those.

The goal of discipline is obedience, and this goal is encouraged in Ephesians 6:1-4. Once again we see this as a key issue for Christians - how we learn obedience to our parents will affect how we learn obedience to God later on. Family life is the learning ground for obedience to God in adult life.

At the same time, it is very difficult to discipline in balance, and we fathers, in seeking obedience from our children, can often be unreasonable with our children under the pretext of demanding obedience. So the instruction to us is not to frustrate or exasperate or iritate or provoke our children and so make them angry - don't stir them along, but bring them up in the discipline and instruction of the Lord. I know there are times when my kids have really got cross with me, and I know I've been guilty of stiring them up.

Deuteronomy 6:1-7. Way back in the days of Moses, God instructed the Israelites to share God's Word in their homes, so that children would grow up in the knowledge of the Lord. Do we spend time with our children, teaching them the Word, praying with them? We need to be giving them that positive input and encouragement each day. I'll pick up this theme next chapter as we consider living as a Christian family today.

6. Understanding Your Child's Personality

In more recent years, the science of human behaviour, mental health and personality has helped us understand certain behaviours much better. Along with this is the need for a more specialised understanding of certain characteristics your child may embrace.

Austism is now commonly used to describe people who exhibit particular behavoural characteristics, and the recognition that behaviour is really a function of how our brains interpret the world around us. Autism includes a range from mild to severe, as well as many different characteristics, which may include ADHD (Attention Deficit Hyerpactivity Disorder). The key thing is that parents understand that because their child's brain interprets the world around differently and can overload quickly, leading to reactionary or aggressive behaviour, standard approaches to discipline need to be adjusted to ones that manage behaviour sensitively.

How to **Make Your Family Strong**

LIVING AS A CHRISTIAN FAMILY TODAY

1. Western based attitudes.

In Melanesia today, and particularly in the towns and cities, people are coming more and more under the influence of western attitudes and lifestyles. Some may have equated western ways with Christian ways, so they think that to embrace western ways means to embrace Christian ways. However, this equation in incorrect. Even western missionaries carry with them what we call "cultural baggage", aspects of their own lifestyle which are western and not necessarily Christian. Non-christian-westerners may demonstrate "good" lifestyles, but more often their lifestyle is in conflict with a truly Biblical lifestyle of devotion to God.

So it is important for Melanesians to understand and critically assess a number of western based attitudes concerning family, marriage and morality, which have crept into society. These attitudes have become assimilated with Christian beliefs, or accepted as Christian responses, when in fact they are in opposition to true Christian ethics.

(a) The Media.

The communication media - magazines, newspapers, radio, particularly TV and cinema - has done much to destroy a true Christian view of morality. Censorship is almost non-existant in most countries these days, and so the degredation, violence and sexually orientated rubbish which is screened is virtually unchecked. It is left to the viewer to respond by either watching or not. However, the lure of the movie and the flicker of the TV screen are things which are very hard to refuse. However, it is essential to learn how to say no to your children, and turn the TV or video off when un-

How to Make Your Family Strong

suitable programs are being shown.

The several areas that affect us most are in the acceptance of violence and a morality which is not from God - eg, adultery, singles sex, homosexuality etc.. There are also dangers from programs which promote (usually very subtley) disrespect for parents and other authorities, including God. Whereas violence and the abuse and disregard for authority are basic issues to consider, in the scope of this book, we will confine ourselves to looking at moral attitudes.

(b) Moral Decay through the Media.

The glamour of beautiful, and usually sexy, women on the TV and movie screen is divorced from the real world. It is a totally unreal world of make believe, fairy tales and stage props, which unfortunately the viewer never sees. It is also one of the most powerful ways in which Satan can influence us. As we watch, we begin to identify with the actors and actresses, and begin to feel involved with them, and suddenly we no longer think of them as actors, but real people in real life situations. *We forget that when the camera stops filming the scene, they pack their bag and catch a taxi home, and become normal people, just like you and I.*

Behind the mass media is a campaign inspired by Satan to bring about total moral collapse in our world today. It is part of Satan's strategy to undermine the reign of God in the world by destroying Christians, and so the area of morality is a is prime target. We have looked at some of the goals in marriage and family life that God aspires us to aim for already - virtues such as monogamy, faithfulness, self-giving love, ministry rather than manipulation, discipline, forgiveness,
life-long commitment and so on. But as we pause to seriously consider the "virtues" that the media is wanting us to believe, we discover that it is the opposite of what God wants that is presented - multiple marriages, unfaithfulness, rebellion, violence, short term commitment ('falling in and out of love'), and so on.

How to Make Your Family Strong

In the cinema and TV, divorce and re-marriage, and "de-facto" marriage (living together but without actually being officially married) are common and acceptable. So is "casual sex" (sleeping with someone outside of marriage) and adultery (sleeping with someone else's marriage partner). The concept of ministry in marriage is replaced by the idea that the individual's feelings of satisfaction are the most important thing - in other words, it is what I can get for myself to feel fulfilled and satisfied that is important, not what I can give to my partner. So sex, wrongly called love, has become something that one tries to "get", and is completely selfish.

Along with all this, TV and movie stars seem to remain free from the personal tensions and emotional distress that this behaviour generates.

At least on the screen, we must realize that they are acting a myth. But when we look at their lives behind the screen and see that some many of them are trying to live that way in real life too, we can see the foolishness of it when we see the despair and emptiness in their lives. That's why so many movie stars have turned to drugs, alcoholism and even suicide to try and dull the pain of turning aside from God's way. Beautiful women, easy sex, lots of money and fame definitely do not bring fulfilment in life - only God in Jesus Christ can do that.

The danger in the media then is that we assume that the way life we see on the screen is the way life should be. That is what the media, and Satan, would like us to believe - but we must understand that it is a fairy tale, or even worse, a nightmare. We must make the TV our servant, so we can turn it off when we need to. Too often we are it's slave!

It is just a short step from the cinema to the disco, and young people need to be reminded too that disco's are prime places for self-enjoyment - everything Satan can offer is there, alcohol, partying, sex and drugs. It is there that the thoughts that come from watching movies are put into action. A Christian has no place at a disco.

(c) What the Bible says.

There are many verses in the Bible that tell us the way that God wants us to think and act, particularly when thinking of marriage and family. We have already looked at several, for example Genesis 2:24 and Mark 10, which are the basis for understanding Christian marriage and the ideals of monogamy, commitment and faithfulness. But as well as stating the ideal, the Bible does speak out firmly on what not to do.

1 Thess. 4:3 says clearly that God's will for us is our sanctification - that we abstain from sexual immorality, and that each person know how to have his or her own spouse, not in lust, but in sanctity and honour.

How to Make Your Family Strong

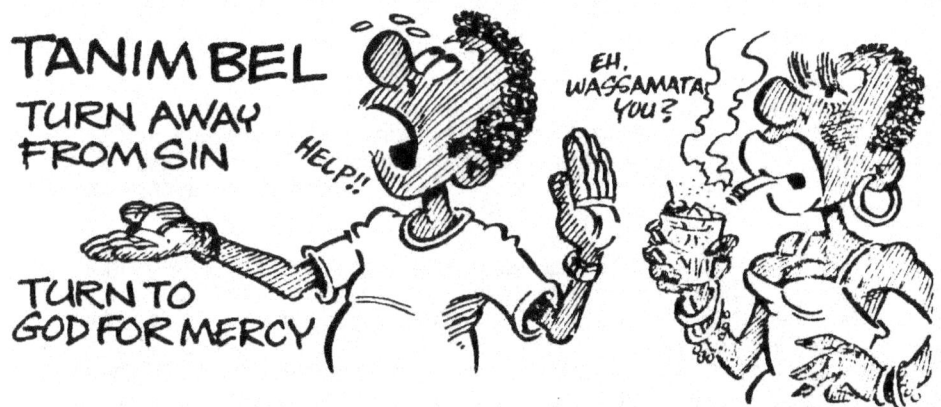

1 Cor. 6:18 - Flee immorality....

1 Cor 7:1 - It is good for a man not to touch a woman...

1 Cor. 6:9...fornicators, nor adulterers nor homosexuals...shall inherit the Kingdom of God.

Proverbs 1 to 7 are full of advise to young men to keep clear of evil women.

The message is clear - the Bible is in clear contrast to the messages that the media would have us believe. It is up to us to decide which we will believe.

2. AIDS and STDs.

AIDS stands for Anti-Immunuity Deficiency Syndrome, and it is something everyone has heard of, but I suspect few really know about. So I have included it in this section that we might be educated to understand it.

AIDS is a killer disease - there is no cure for it, and it is probable that it will be many years before there is a cure, if ever. It comes under the broad category of being an STD (Sexually Transmitted Disease), though does have differences to other STDs. Whereas other STDs cause illness with symptoms such as sores, AIDS attacks the body's natural ability to fight off sickness, it's immunity system, and so leaves the victim helpless and weak to survive even relatively minor illnesses such as chest infections or colds. The patient dies not from the direct AIDS virus, but because he or she can no longer fight off other sicknesses, which then kill him/her.

How to Make Your Family Strong

The AIDS virus is transmitted in body fluids only, particularly blood and internal body fluids. There are several ways that it can be recieved, such as through using a needle used on or by someone infected, or receiving a blood transfusion from an infected person, or through sexual activity with an infected person. Many people would see AIDS as God's judgement on a fallen world, where all sorts of sexual perversions have allowed this disease to spread. *(Romans 1)*.

One of the tragic things that has resulted from the AIDS scare is that instead of the community worldwide acting to stop this disease spreading, Satan has used it to actually promote ungodly sexual activity. *The only effective way to stop AIDS is to halt all ungodly sexual activity and return to God's way* - no sexual activity outside of marriage. If AIDS (and any STD, for that matter) is transmitted through multiple partner sexual activity, then it will not be transmitted between two people who have known no other partner.

Unfortunately the advertising and educational programs are saying that condoms are the answer. This does not address the basic problem, though, which is the problem of immorality. So people are being led to believe that it is okay to continue in their sexual activity, when they must be told to stop it.

Christians, we have to shout loud and clear that there is only one solution to AIDS and other STDs, and that is to return to God's way.

3. Family Devotional Life.

We turn now to consider some more positive aspects of living as a Christian Family today, particularly devotional life. Needless to say, maintaining a constant devotional life in your family will continue to be one of the most difficult things you will do. Satan is active to rob us of our joy and freedom in the Lord, and he will continue to tell us that other activities should take priority over devotions, assail us with distractions, frustrate us with disinterest, and steal our consistancy. However, perseverance is required in most aspects of living as a Christian today, and in this matter no less.

(a) Parents.

We seen in earlier studies how important it is for children to learn from their parents, and in spiritual growth they will also learn much. How you respect and treat the Word of God will determine in many respects what your children think of it as they grow up. How they see you pray and spend your time in devotions will set them an example to strive after. Your children may not see you every time you go to pray, but they will see the effect of it on your life and in the life of the family. Pray each day

How to Make Your Family Strong

for your children, and you will begin to see God at work releasing in them His transforming power. Pray daily with your children also, for they will not only learn how to pray from you, but will find strength and encouragement from your prayer.

As we pray with our kids, we can help prayer to become a natural part of their lives, so that they learn from us how to keep in tune with God.

If we have not developed our own walk with the Lord, though, we will not be able to pass on anything worthwhile to our children, because they see through anything that is not genuine. Spend time each day with the Lord, but don't make it such a law that you continually live in guilt because you missed out one day. But set a pattern of time each day with the Lord - reading the Bible, a helpful Christian book; praising Him in song or quiet worship; waiting on Him to hear His voice to you today; praying for your own needs, those of your family, and the world around you. Cultivate your own friendship with Jesus, remembering that we are part of God's family, and He wants us to relate to Him with all the spontinaity and freedom that a family embraces.

Husbands and wives, learn to share and pray together, about every- thing. Then support and encourage eachother in prayer and ministry, building up eachother. Your success as Christian parents will be the fruit of your relationship together.

(b) Children.

Encourage your children to participate in devotional exercises. Children can know the Lord and respond to Him from a very young age, but we have the responsibility to help them mature as they grow, to give them substance to the expression of their faith. Much of what we do with them as youngsters is teaching them - how to pray, how to read the Bible, how to approach the Scriptures and interpret them, and so on. It is so easy to give up family devotions. We must keep before us our goal - which is that our children learn how to maintain an effective communication with the Lord by themselves as they grow up.

John and Paula Sandford, in their book *"Restoring the Christian Family"*, have a diagram (next page) which helps us see the outworking of spiritual nurture, starting with Spirit Oneness (turning to the Lord), then Soul Oneness (ministering to eachother), and then incorporating ministry to one's children, and on to the church and world.

We live in a secular world with so many influences that are designed to turn us away from God that we must maintain something in our daily lives which provides an anchor for us, to stop us being washed away.

How to **Make Your Family Strong**

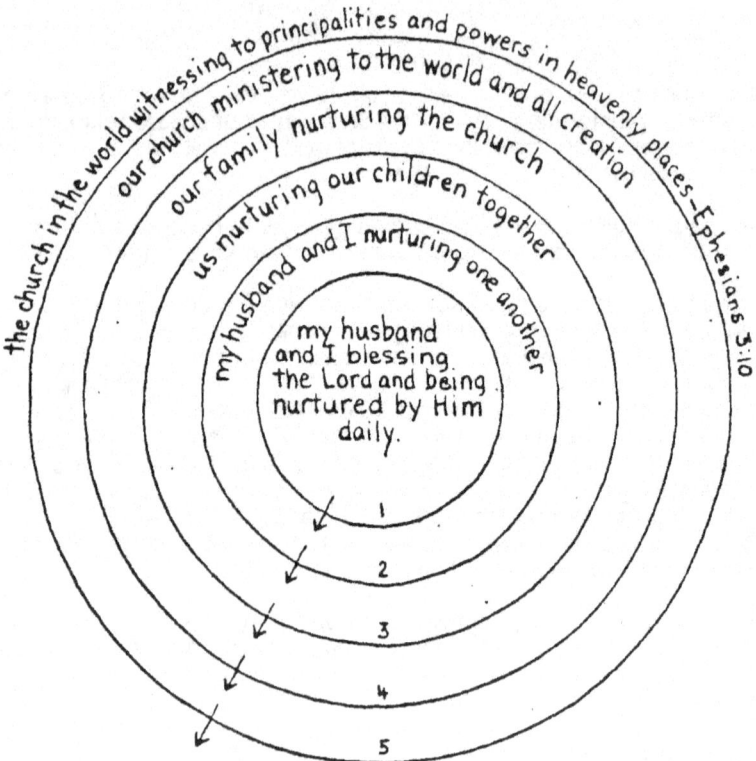

At each level, whether personal, for couples, or within the family, time aside with the Lord is essential. This is a time to draw back from the world and draw from the resources of Christ and the Holy Spirit. It is a time when we say very clearly to God and to eachother that God is number One in our lives.

When Joshua was getting ready to die, he gathered the Isrealites together and reminded them of the many things God had done for them in bringing them into the Promised Land. But, just as we are today, the Israelites were faced with compromising their faith as a result of ungodly influences around them. Josua (*Joshua 24:15*) challenges them again to consider where their hearts and loyalties are.

"If it is disagreeable in your sight to serve the Lord, choose for yourselves today whom you will serve.....but as for me and my house, we will serve the Lord." Today in Melanesia, and throughout the world, this is a challenge that comes back to us. It is my prayer that each of us might return the challenge and the palaces of heaven and hell will resound with our reply - **"as for me and my house, we will serve the Lord."**

How to Make Your Family Strong

Bibliography and further reading

Crabb Jr.,Lawrence, 1984, *The Marriage Builder*, S.John Bacon.

Dobson, Dr.James, 1976, *Dare to Discipline*, Tyndale House.

Fountain, O.C., 1985, *Marriage the Melanesian Way*, CBM.

Fountain, Ossie & Jennie, 1986, *Marriage is for Life*, CBM.

Malins, Ian, 1987, *Christian Marriage & Family Life*, CBM.

Price, Dr.David J.,1984, *The Two shall become One*, CBM.

Prince, J.R., 1981, *Boy meets Girl*, CBM.

Sandford, John & Paula, 1986, *Restoring the Christian Family*, Victory House.

Schaeffer, Edith, 1975, *What is a Family*, Highlands Books.

Trobisch, Walter, 1976, *I Married You*, Inter-Varsity Press.

Trobisch, Walter, 1981, *I Loved a Girl*, Inter-Varsity Press.

Note: Most of the books published by CBM (Christian Books Melanesia) are also available in Tok Pisin.

How to Make Your Family Strong

Discussion Questions

Chapter 1 - God's Design in Marriage & Family.

1. Why did God make mankind different from the rest of creation? What was God's intention for mankind?

2. Does your (cultural) view of marriage reflect the BIble's model of "leaving, cleaving and becoming one flesh"?

3. Why is a wedding important and what does it mean in your culture traditionally? What about in modern society?

4. Which of the key truths on pages 6 and 7 help you understand why marriage is so important in God's eyes?

Chapter 2 - The Ideal of Marriage.

1. If the relationship between Jesus and His Church is the example, discuss the ways in which husbands should relate to their wives, and wives to their husbands. (Refer to the diagram on page 20). Is that different to what happens now? What needs to change?

2. Which of the three points of the marriage diagram is weakest in your marriage relationship? What can you do to strengthen it now?

3. What words express what should be the basis for our marriage relationship? How can you apply those more in your own marriage?

4. If you have had failings in relationships, can you go back and undo mistakes? As a Christian, what pathway is there for us to try again?

How to Make Your Family Strong

Chapter 3 - Husbands and Wives.

1. How can you describe our needs in these three areas:
physical -
security -
security -
What needs do you personally have in any of these areas?

2. Why do we often not find these needs met by our marriage partner? What one word describes our atitude?

3. What does Christ offer us so that can change our marriage relationship?

4. Discuss ways that you may have been manipulating your marriage partner. How can you change that to minster to them now?

5. In the definition in the diagram on page 20, how is submitting to authority in the Bible different to wordly ideas about responding to authority? How can that be applied to a marriage relationship?

Chapter 4 - Children in the Family.

1. What are some reasons why a woman may not conceinve a child? Is it always the woman's fault?

2. Is every child a gift from God? How should children conceived outside of the marriage triangle relationship be regarded? Should they be discarded? What does the Bible say about this?

3. Why do parents sometimes become angry when trying to discipline their child? How should discipline be administered? How can you do this better?

How to Make Your Family Strong

Chapter 5 - Living as a Christian Family Today.

1. How much influence does the media have in your daily life? Do you find yourself watching things on media such as facebook and other internet sites that you know are a compromise to your time and faith? What one thing could you do to reduce that influence?

2. Do you agree that there is a dedicated effort by God's enemies to corrupt Christians through the media? How have you experienced that yourself?

3. Why do you think that sexual temptation is such a big target by God's enemies? What are some of the negative results from allowing this temptation to take hold in a person's life? How can that be reversed?

4. Why is it important for parents to have a regular devotional life and share together? What can you do in your family times to develop a devotional life in your children as well?

www.ingramcontent.com/pod-product-compliance
Lightning Source LLC
Chambersburg PA
CBHW072339300426
44109CB00042B/1953